50 Hispanic Smoothie Dishes

By: Kelly Johnson

Table of Contents

- Mango Lassi
- Horchata Smoothie
- Guava and Pineapple Smoothie
- Papaya and Coconut Smoothie
- Tamarind Smoothie
- Spicy Mango Smoothie
- Avocado Smoothie
- Pineapple and Cucumber Smoothie
- Strawberry Agua Fresca Smoothie
- Watermelon and Lime Smoothie
- Pina Colada Smoothie
- Dragon Fruit Smoothie
- Cantaloupe and Lime Smoothie
- Mexican Chocolate Smoothie
- Chia and Mango Smoothie
- Hibiscus and Berry Smoothie
- Cinnamon and Banana Smoothie
- Sweet Corn and Coconut Smoothie
- Banana and Peanut Butter Smoothie
- Passion Fruit Smoothie
- Choco-Tamarind Smoothie
- Papaya and Mango Smoothie
- Sweet Plantain Smoothie
- Lime and Mint Smoothie
- Guava and Coconut Smoothie
- Blueberry and Pomegranate Smoothie
- Raspberry and Hibiscus Smoothie
- Mango and Pineapple Smoothie
- Cinnamon Horchata Smoothie
- Green Chile and Pineapple Smoothie
- Lemon and Watermelon Smoothie
- Blackberry and Lime Smoothie
- Spicy Tamarind Smoothie
- Melon and Cucumber Smoothie
- Strawberry and Coconut Smoothie

- Coconut and Papaya Smoothie
- Lime and Mango Smoothie
- Mixed Berry and Hibiscus Smoothie
- Grape and Coconut Smoothie
- Pear and Cinnamon Smoothie
- Watermelon and Mint Smoothie
- Strawberry and Mango Smoothie
- Coconut and Sweet Plantain Smoothie
- Spicy Pineapple Smoothie
- Dragon Fruit and Banana Smoothie
- Pineapple and Chia Smoothie
- Lime and Coconut Smoothie
- Avocado and Strawberry Smoothie
- Jugo de Naranja Smoothie
- Pineapple and Guava Smoothie

Mango Lassi

Ingredients:

- 1 cup fresh mango, diced
- 1/2 cup plain yogurt
- 1/2 cup milk (or almond milk)
- 1 tablespoon honey or sugar (optional)
- 1/4 teaspoon ground cardamom (optional)
- Ice cubes

Instructions:

1. Add the mango, yogurt, milk, honey (if using), and ground cardamom (if using) to a blender.
2. Blend until smooth. Add ice cubes and blend again if you want a colder, thicker smoothie.
3. Pour into glasses and serve immediately.

Horchata Smoothie

Ingredients:

- 1/2 cup rice (soaked for 4 hours or overnight)
- 1/4 cup almonds
- 1/4 teaspoon cinnamon
- 1 tablespoon vanilla extract
- 2 cups water
- 1/2 cup milk (or almond milk)
- 1 tablespoon sugar or to taste
- Ice cubes

Instructions:

1. Drain the soaked rice and almonds. Add them to a blender with cinnamon, vanilla extract, and water.
2. Blend until smooth. Strain the mixture through a fine sieve or cheesecloth to remove any solids.
3. Return the strained liquid to the blender and add milk and sugar. Blend until well combined.
4. Add ice cubes to the blender and blend again for a chilled smoothie.
5. Pour into glasses and serve.

Guava and Pineapple Smoothie

Ingredients:

- 1 cup fresh guava, peeled and chopped
- 1/2 cup fresh pineapple, chopped
- 1/2 cup coconut water
- 1/2 cup Greek yogurt or coconut yogurt
- 1 tablespoon honey (optional)
- Ice cubes

Instructions:

1. Add the guava, pineapple, coconut water, Greek yogurt (or coconut yogurt), and honey (if using) to a blender.
2. Blend until smooth. Add ice cubes and blend again to chill the smoothie.
3. Pour into glasses and serve immediately.

Papaya and Coconut Smoothie

Ingredients:

- 1 cup fresh papaya, peeled and chopped
- 1/2 cup coconut milk
- 1/2 cup orange juice
- 1 tablespoon honey (optional)
- Ice cubes

Instructions:

1. Add the papaya, coconut milk, orange juice, and honey (if using) to a blender.
2. Blend until smooth and creamy. Add ice cubes and blend again to chill.
3. Pour into glasses and serve.

Tamarind Smoothie

Ingredients:

- 1/4 cup tamarind pulp
- 1 tablespoon honey or sugar
- 1/2 cup orange juice
- 1/2 cup water
- Ice cubes

Instructions:

1. In a small bowl, soak the tamarind pulp in warm water for 10-15 minutes. Strain to remove seeds and fibers, leaving only the tamarind juice.
2. Add the tamarind juice, honey (or sugar), orange juice, and water to a blender.
3. Blend until smooth and add ice cubes. Blend again to chill the smoothie.
4. Pour into glasses and serve.

Spicy Mango Smoothie

Ingredients:

- 1 cup fresh mango, diced
- 1/2 teaspoon chili powder (or to taste)
- 1/4 teaspoon cayenne pepper (optional)
- 1 tablespoon honey or agave syrup
- 1/2 cup Greek yogurt or coconut yogurt
- 1/2 cup coconut water
- Ice cubes

Instructions:

1. Add the mango, chili powder, cayenne pepper (if using), honey, yogurt, and coconut water to a blender.
2. Blend until smooth. Add ice cubes and blend again for a chilled smoothie.
3. Pour into glasses and serve immediately.

Avocado Smoothie

Ingredients:

- 1 ripe avocado
- 1/2 cup milk (or almond milk)
- 1/2 cup Greek yogurt or coconut yogurt
- 1 tablespoon honey (optional)
- 1/2 teaspoon vanilla extract
- Ice cubes

Instructions:

1. Scoop the avocado flesh into a blender. Add the milk, yogurt, honey (if using), and vanilla extract.
2. Blend until smooth and creamy. Add ice cubes for a chilled smoothie and blend again.
3. Pour into glasses and serve.

Pineapple and Cucumber Smoothie

Ingredients:

- 1/2 cup fresh pineapple, chopped
- 1/2 cucumber, peeled and chopped
- 1/2 cup coconut water
- 1 tablespoon lime juice
- Ice cubes

Instructions:

1. Add the pineapple, cucumber, coconut water, and lime juice to a blender.
2. Blend until smooth. Add ice cubes and blend again for a chilled smoothie.
3. Pour into glasses and serve immediately.

Strawberry Agua Fresca Smoothie

Ingredients:

- 1 cup fresh strawberries, hulled
- 1 tablespoon lime juice
- 1 tablespoon honey or sugar
- 1 cup water
- Ice cubes

Instructions:

1. Add the strawberries, lime juice, honey (or sugar), and water to a blender.
2. Blend until smooth. Add ice cubes and blend again for a chilled smoothie.
3. Pour into glasses and serve immediately.

Watermelon and Lime Smoothie

Ingredients:

- 2 cups fresh watermelon, chopped
- 1 tablespoon lime juice
- 1 teaspoon honey or agave syrup (optional)
- 1/2 cup coconut water or regular water
- Ice cubes

Instructions:

1. Add the watermelon, lime juice, honey (if using), and coconut water to a blender.
2. Blend until smooth. Add ice cubes and blend again for a chilled smoothie.
3. Pour into glasses and serve immediately.

Pina Colada Smoothie

Ingredients:

- 1 cup fresh pineapple, chopped
- 1/2 cup coconut milk
- 1/2 cup Greek yogurt (or coconut yogurt)
- 1 tablespoon honey or agave syrup (optional)
- 1/2 teaspoon vanilla extract
- Ice cubes

Instructions:

1. Add the pineapple, coconut milk, yogurt, honey (if using), and vanilla extract to a blender.
2. Blend until smooth. Add ice cubes and blend again for a thicker, chilled smoothie.
3. Pour into glasses and serve immediately.

Dragon Fruit Smoothie

Ingredients:

- 1 cup dragon fruit (pitaya), peeled and chopped
- 1/2 banana
- 1/2 cup coconut water
- 1/2 cup Greek yogurt or coconut yogurt
- 1 tablespoon honey (optional)
- Ice cubes

Instructions:

1. Add the dragon fruit, banana, coconut water, yogurt, and honey (if using) to a blender.
2. Blend until smooth. Add ice cubes and blend again for a chilled smoothie.
3. Pour into glasses and serve immediately.

Cantaloupe and Lime Smoothie

Ingredients:

- 1 cup cantaloupe, chopped
- 1 tablespoon lime juice
- 1/2 cup coconut water
- 1/2 teaspoon honey or agave syrup (optional)
- Ice cubes

Instructions:

1. Add the cantaloupe, lime juice, coconut water, and honey (if using) to a blender.
2. Blend until smooth. Add ice cubes and blend again for a chilled smoothie.
3. Pour into glasses and serve immediately.

Mexican Chocolate Smoothie

Ingredients:

- 1/2 banana
- 1 tablespoon unsweetened cocoa powder
- 1/2 teaspoon cinnamon
- 1/4 teaspoon chili powder (optional)
- 1 cup almond milk (or regular milk)
- 1 tablespoon honey or agave syrup
- Ice cubes

Instructions:

1. Add the banana, cocoa powder, cinnamon, chili powder (if using), almond milk, and honey to a blender.
2. Blend until smooth. Add ice cubes and blend again for a chilled, thicker smoothie.
3. Pour into glasses and serve immediately.

Chia and Mango Smoothie

Ingredients:

- 1 cup fresh mango, chopped
- 1 tablespoon chia seeds
- 1/2 cup coconut water
- 1/2 cup Greek yogurt or coconut yogurt
- 1 tablespoon honey (optional)
- Ice cubes

Instructions:

1. Add the mango, chia seeds, coconut water, yogurt, and honey (if using) to a blender.
2. Blend until smooth. Let the smoothie sit for a minute to allow the chia seeds to absorb liquid and thicken.
3. Add ice cubes and blend again for a chilled smoothie.
4. Pour into glasses and serve immediately.

Hibiscus and Berry Smoothie

Ingredients:

- 1/2 cup dried hibiscus petals (or 1 cup brewed hibiscus tea, cooled)
- 1/2 cup mixed berries (strawberries, blueberries, raspberries)
- 1 tablespoon honey or agave syrup (optional)
- 1/2 cup water or coconut water
- Ice cubes

Instructions:

1. Brew hibiscus tea and let it cool, or use dried hibiscus petals and steep them in hot water for 5-10 minutes, then cool.
2. Add the hibiscus tea, mixed berries, honey (if using), and water to a blender.
3. Blend until smooth. Add ice cubes and blend again for a chilled smoothie.
4. Pour into glasses and serve.

Cinnamon and Banana Smoothie

Ingredients:

- 1 ripe banana
- 1/2 teaspoon ground cinnamon
- 1 tablespoon almond butter or peanut butter (optional)
- 1/2 cup milk (or almond milk)
- 1 tablespoon honey or agave syrup (optional)
- Ice cubes

Instructions:

1. Add the banana, cinnamon, almond butter (if using), milk, and honey (if using) to a blender.
2. Blend until smooth. Add ice cubes and blend again for a chilled smoothie.
3. Pour into glasses and serve immediately.

Sweet Corn and Coconut Smoothie

Ingredients:

- 1/2 cup cooked sweet corn kernels (cooled)
- 1/2 cup coconut milk
- 1 tablespoon honey or agave syrup
- 1/2 teaspoon vanilla extract
- 1/2 cup ice cubes

Instructions:

1. Add the sweet corn, coconut milk, honey, vanilla extract, and ice cubes to a blender.
2. Blend until smooth and creamy.
3. Pour into glasses and serve immediately.

Banana and Peanut Butter Smoothie

Ingredients:

- 1 ripe banana
- 2 tablespoons peanut butter
- 1/2 cup milk (or almond milk)
- 1 tablespoon honey or maple syrup (optional)
- 1/2 teaspoon cinnamon (optional)
- Ice cubes

Instructions:

1. Add the banana, peanut butter, milk, honey (if using), and cinnamon (if using) to a blender.
2. Blend until smooth and creamy. Add ice cubes and blend again for a chilled smoothie.
3. Pour into glasses and serve immediately.

Passion Fruit Smoothie

Ingredients:

- 2 ripe passion fruits, scooped out
- 1/2 cup pineapple or orange juice
- 1 tablespoon honey or agave syrup (optional)
- 1/2 cup Greek yogurt or coconut yogurt
- Ice cubes

Instructions:

1. Add the passion fruit pulp, juice, honey (if using), and yogurt to a blender.
2. Blend until smooth. Add ice cubes and blend again for a chilled smoothie.
3. Pour into glasses and serve immediately.

Choco-Tamarind Smoothie

Ingredients:

- 1 tablespoon tamarind pulp (or tamarind concentrate)
- 1 tablespoon unsweetened cocoa powder
- 1/2 cup milk (or almond milk)
- 1 tablespoon honey or maple syrup
- 1/4 teaspoon ground cinnamon
- Ice cubes

Instructions:

1. Add the tamarind pulp, cocoa powder, milk, honey, cinnamon, and ice cubes to a blender.
2. Blend until smooth.
3. Pour into glasses and serve immediately.

Papaya and Mango Smoothie

Ingredients:

- 1/2 cup fresh papaya, chopped
- 1/2 cup fresh mango, chopped
- 1/2 cup coconut water
- 1 tablespoon honey or agave syrup (optional)
- 1/2 cup ice cubes

Instructions:

1. Add the papaya, mango, coconut water, honey (if using), and ice cubes to a blender.
2. Blend until smooth.
3. Pour into glasses and serve immediately.

Sweet Plantain Smoothie

Ingredients:

- 1 ripe plantain, peeled and sliced
- 1/2 cup milk (or almond milk)
- 1 tablespoon honey or agave syrup
- 1/2 teaspoon vanilla extract
- Ice cubes

Instructions:

1. Add the plantain, milk, honey, vanilla extract, and ice cubes to a blender.
2. Blend until smooth and creamy.
3. Pour into glasses and serve immediately.

Lime and Mint Smoothie

Ingredients:

- 1/2 cup fresh lime juice (about 2 limes)
- 1/2 cup fresh mint leaves
- 1 tablespoon honey or agave syrup (optional)
- 1/2 cup water or coconut water
- Ice cubes

Instructions:

1. Add the lime juice, mint leaves, honey (if using), water, and ice cubes to a blender.
2. Blend until smooth and refreshing.
3. Pour into glasses and serve immediately.

Guava and Coconut Smoothie

Ingredients:

- 1 ripe guava, peeled and chopped
- 1/2 cup coconut milk
- 1/2 cup Greek yogurt or coconut yogurt
- 1 tablespoon honey or agave syrup (optional)
- 1/2 cup ice cubes

Instructions:

1. Add the guava, coconut milk, yogurt, honey (if using), and ice cubes to a blender.
2. Blend until smooth.
3. Pour into glasses and serve immediately.

Blueberry and Pomegranate Smoothie

Ingredients:

- 1/2 cup blueberries (fresh or frozen)
- 1/2 cup pomegranate seeds
- 1/2 cup Greek yogurt or coconut yogurt
- 1 tablespoon honey or agave syrup (optional)
- 1/2 cup water or coconut water
- Ice cubes

Instructions:

1. Add the blueberries, pomegranate seeds, yogurt, honey (if using), and water to a blender.
2. Blend until smooth. Add ice cubes and blend again for a chilled smoothie.
3. Pour into glasses and serve immediately.

Raspberry and Hibiscus Smoothie

Ingredients:

- 1/2 cup fresh or frozen raspberries
- 1/2 cup hibiscus tea (cooled)
- 1 tablespoon honey or agave syrup (optional)
- 1/2 cup Greek yogurt or coconut yogurt
- Ice cubes

Instructions:

1. Brew hibiscus tea and let it cool.
2. Add the raspberries, hibiscus tea, honey (if using), and yogurt to a blender.
3. Blend until smooth. Add ice cubes and blend again for a chilled smoothie.
4. Pour into glasses and serve immediately.

Mango and Pineapple Smoothie

Ingredients:

- 1/2 cup fresh mango, chopped
- 1/2 cup fresh pineapple, chopped
- 1/2 cup coconut water or juice
- 1 tablespoon honey or agave syrup (optional)
- Ice cubes

Instructions:

1. Add the mango, pineapple, coconut water (or juice), and honey (if using) to a blender.
2. Blend until smooth and creamy. Add ice cubes and blend again for a chilled smoothie.
3. Pour into glasses and serve immediately.

Cinnamon Horchata Smoothie

Ingredients:

- 1/2 cup rice milk (or regular milk)
- 1/4 cup cooked rice (cooled)
- 1/4 teaspoon cinnamon
- 1 tablespoon honey or agave syrup
- 1/2 cup ice cubes

Instructions:

1. Add the rice milk, cooked rice, cinnamon, honey, and ice cubes to a blender.
2. Blend until smooth and creamy.
3. Pour into glasses and serve immediately with a sprinkle of cinnamon on top.

Green Chile and Pineapple Smoothie

Ingredients:

- 1/2 cup fresh pineapple, chopped
- 1 small green chile (seeds removed, finely chopped)
- 1/2 cup coconut water or juice
- 1 tablespoon honey or agave syrup (optional)
- Ice cubes

Instructions:

1. Add the pineapple, green chile, coconut water (or juice), and honey (if using) to a blender.
2. Blend until smooth and slightly spicy. Add ice cubes and blend again for a chilled smoothie.
3. Pour into glasses and serve immediately.

Lemon and Watermelon Smoothie

Ingredients:

- 1 cup fresh watermelon, cubed
- 1/2 lemon, juiced
- 1 tablespoon honey or agave syrup (optional)
- 1/2 cup coconut water
- Ice cubes

Instructions:

1. Add the watermelon, lemon juice, honey (if using), coconut water, and ice cubes to a blender.
2. Blend until smooth and refreshing.
3. Pour into glasses and serve immediately.

Blackberry and Lime Smoothie

Ingredients:

- 1/2 cup fresh or frozen blackberries
- 1/2 lime, juiced
- 1 tablespoon honey or agave syrup (optional)
- 1/2 cup Greek yogurt or coconut yogurt
- Ice cubes

Instructions:

1. Add the blackberries, lime juice, honey (if using), yogurt, and ice cubes to a blender.
2. Blend until smooth and creamy.
3. Pour into glasses and serve immediately.

Spicy Tamarind Smoothie

Ingredients:

- 1 tablespoon tamarind pulp (or tamarind concentrate)
- 1/2 teaspoon ground chili powder (or to taste)
- 1/2 cup coconut milk
- 1 tablespoon honey or agave syrup (optional)
- Ice cubes

Instructions:

1. Add the tamarind pulp, chili powder, coconut milk, honey (if using), and ice cubes to a blender.
2. Blend until smooth.
3. Pour into glasses and serve immediately for a tangy and spicy smoothie.

Melon and Cucumber Smoothie

Ingredients:

- 1/2 cup cantaloupe or honeydew melon, chopped
- 1/2 cucumber, peeled and chopped
- 1/2 cup coconut water
- 1 tablespoon honey or agave syrup (optional)
- Ice cubes

Instructions:

1. Add the melon, cucumber, coconut water, honey (if using), and ice cubes to a blender.
2. Blend until smooth and refreshing.
3. Pour into glasses and serve immediately.

Strawberry and Coconut Smoothie

Ingredients:

- 1/2 cup fresh or frozen strawberries
- 1/2 cup coconut milk
- 1 tablespoon honey or agave syrup (optional)
- 1/2 cup Greek yogurt or coconut yogurt
- Ice cubes

Instructions:

1. Add the strawberries, coconut milk, honey (if using), yogurt, and ice cubes to a blender.
2. Blend until smooth and creamy.
3. Pour into glasses and serve immediately.

Coconut and Papaya Smoothie

Ingredients:

- 1/2 cup fresh papaya, chopped
- 1/2 cup coconut milk
- 1 tablespoon honey or agave syrup (optional)
- 1/2 cup ice cubes
- 1/4 teaspoon vanilla extract (optional)

Instructions:

1. Add the papaya, coconut milk, honey (if using), ice cubes, and vanilla extract (if using) to a blender.
2. Blend until smooth and creamy.
3. Pour into glasses and serve immediately for a tropical, refreshing smoothie.

Lime and Mango Smoothie

Ingredients:

- 1/2 cup fresh mango, chopped
- 1/2 lime, juiced
- 1/2 cup coconut water or juice
- 1 tablespoon honey or agave syrup (optional)
- Ice cubes

Instructions:

1. Add the mango, lime juice, coconut water (or juice), honey (if using), and ice cubes to a blender.
2. Blend until smooth and refreshing.
3. Pour into glasses and serve immediately.

Mixed Berry and Hibiscus Smoothie

Ingredients:

- 1/2 cup mixed berries (strawberries, blueberries, raspberries)
- 1/2 cup hibiscus tea (cooled)
- 1 tablespoon honey or agave syrup (optional)
- 1/2 cup Greek yogurt or coconut yogurt
- Ice cubes

Instructions:

1. Brew hibiscus tea and let it cool.
2. Add the mixed berries, hibiscus tea, honey (if using), yogurt, and ice cubes to a blender.
3. Blend until smooth and creamy.
4. Pour into glasses and serve immediately.

Grape and Coconut Smoothie

Ingredients:

- 1/2 cup green or red grapes
- 1/2 cup coconut milk
- 1 tablespoon honey or agave syrup (optional)
- 1/2 cup Greek yogurt or coconut yogurt
- Ice cubes

Instructions:

1. Add the grapes, coconut milk, honey (if using), yogurt, and ice cubes to a blender.
2. Blend until smooth and creamy.
3. Pour into glasses and serve immediately.

Pear and Cinnamon Smoothie

Ingredients:

- 1 ripe pear, chopped
- 1/4 teaspoon ground cinnamon
- 1/2 cup almond milk or milk of choice
- 1 tablespoon honey or agave syrup (optional)
- Ice cubes

Instructions:

1. Add the pear, cinnamon, almond milk (or your choice of milk), honey (if using), and ice cubes to a blender.
2. Blend until smooth and creamy.
3. Pour into glasses and serve immediately for a warm, comforting smoothie.

Watermelon and Mint Smoothie

Ingredients:

- 1 cup fresh watermelon, chopped
- 1 tablespoon fresh mint leaves
- 1/2 lime, juiced
- 1 tablespoon honey or agave syrup (optional)
- Ice cubes

Instructions:

1. Add the watermelon, mint leaves, lime juice, honey (if using), and ice cubes to a blender.
2. Blend until smooth and refreshing.
3. Pour into glasses and serve immediately for a cooling, minty smoothie.

Strawberry and Mango Smoothie

Ingredients:

- 1/2 cup fresh strawberries, chopped
- 1/2 cup fresh mango, chopped
- 1/2 cup orange juice
- 1 tablespoon honey or agave syrup (optional)
- Ice cubes

Instructions:

1. Add the strawberries, mango, orange juice, honey (if using), and ice cubes to a blender.
2. Blend until smooth and creamy.
3. Pour into glasses and serve immediately for a sweet, fruity smoothie.

Coconut and Sweet Plantain Smoothie

Ingredients:

- 1 ripe plantain, peeled and chopped
- 1/2 cup coconut milk
- 1 tablespoon honey or agave syrup (optional)
- 1/2 teaspoon vanilla extract (optional)
- Ice cubes

Instructions:

1. Add the chopped plantain, coconut milk, honey (if using), vanilla extract (if using), and ice cubes to a blender.
2. Blend until smooth and creamy.
3. Pour into glasses and serve immediately for a creamy, tropical treat.

Spicy Pineapple Smoothie

Ingredients:

- 1/2 cup fresh pineapple, chopped
- 1/2 cup coconut water
- 1/2 teaspoon chili powder or cayenne pepper
- 1 tablespoon honey or agave syrup (optional)
- Ice cubes

Instructions:

1. Add the pineapple, coconut water, chili powder or cayenne pepper, honey (if using), and ice cubes to a blender.
2. Blend until smooth and spicy.
3. Pour into glasses and serve immediately for a tropical smoothie with a kick.

Dragon Fruit and Banana Smoothie

Ingredients:

- 1/2 cup dragon fruit (pitaya), chopped
- 1 banana
- 1/2 cup coconut milk
- 1 tablespoon honey or agave syrup (optional)
- Ice cubes

Instructions:

1. Add the dragon fruit, banana, coconut milk, honey (if using), and ice cubes to a blender.
2. Blend until smooth and creamy.
3. Pour into glasses and serve immediately for a colorful and refreshing smoothie.

Pineapple and Chia Smoothie

Ingredients:

- 1/2 cup fresh pineapple, chopped
- 1 tablespoon chia seeds
- 1/2 cup coconut water or almond milk
- 1 tablespoon honey or agave syrup (optional)
- Ice cubes

Instructions:

1. Add the pineapple, chia seeds, coconut water (or almond milk), honey (if using), and ice cubes to a blender.
2. Blend until smooth and creamy.
3. Pour into glasses and serve immediately for a nutritious, hydrating smoothie.

Lime and Coconut Smoothie

Ingredients:

- 1/2 cup coconut milk
- 1/2 lime, juiced
- 1 tablespoon honey or agave syrup (optional)
- 1/4 teaspoon shredded coconut (optional)
- Ice cubes

Instructions:

1. Add the coconut milk, lime juice, honey (if using), shredded coconut (if using), and ice cubes to a blender.
2. Blend until smooth and refreshing.
3. Pour into glasses and serve immediately for a tropical and zesty smoothie.

Avocado and Strawberry Smoothie

Ingredients:

- 1/2 ripe avocado
- 1/2 cup fresh strawberries, chopped
- 1/2 cup almond milk or milk of choice
- 1 tablespoon honey or agave syrup (optional)
- Ice cubes

Instructions:

1. Add the avocado, strawberries, almond milk (or your choice of milk), honey (if using), and ice cubes to a blender.
2. Blend until smooth and creamy.
3. Pour into glasses and serve immediately for a rich, creamy smoothie.

Jugo de Naranja Smoothie

Ingredients:

- 1 large orange, peeled and segmented
- 1/2 cup Greek yogurt or coconut yogurt
- 1 tablespoon honey or agave syrup (optional)
- Ice cubes

Instructions:

1. Add the orange segments, yogurt, honey (if using), and ice cubes to a blender.
2. Blend until smooth and creamy.
3. Pour into glasses and serve immediately for a refreshing, citrusy smoothie.

Pineapple and Guava Smoothie

Ingredients:

- 1/2 cup fresh pineapple, chopped
- 1/2 cup guava, chopped
- 1/2 cup coconut water
- 1 tablespoon honey or agave syrup (optional)
- Ice cubes

Instructions:

1. Add the pineapple, guava, coconut water, honey (if using), and ice cubes to a blender.
2. Blend until smooth and tropical.
3. Pour into glasses and serve immediately for a deliciously exotic smoothie.

www.ingramcontent.com/pod-product-compliance
Lightning Source LLC
LaVergne TN
LVHW081339060526
838201LV00055B/2736